Meditate by Nature

FOR THOSE TIMES WHEN YOU SEEK SOLID GROUND

Authored by Dr. Bonnie Howard Howell

Photographs by Charlotte Brahm

ISBN: 1475218079
ISBN-13: 9781475218077

Acknowledgements

THIS BOOK WOULD not have come to fruition without the help and support of our friends and family.

We thank our beta readers, Ruth Ann Shannon, Helen Gibson and Dusty Hellmann, for their tremendous insight, patience and targeted suggestions. Thanks to my mother, Betty Howard, and my children Carolyn, Kate and Elaine, for their constant encouragement and support of this project.

A very big, thank you to our editor-in-chief, Barbara Warland, who lovingly, patiently, but firmly corrected my grammar, spelling, sentence structure, etc. As Charlotte says, without Barbara, I would reign supreme as the run-on sentence queen.

My personal thanks to Charlotte for her wonderful eye behind the camera; her talent is without equal. My words followed her photographs, but only after they captured my heart and soul.

Why

W E ARE QUITE frequently asked how this project started and why it took this particular form. My friend, Charlotte, is a talented artist whose medium is photography. She sees things in the world to photograph that bear important messages. As I mentioned, her art inspires the words I write. We are students of nature, and the pictures, words and inspiration for this project were gifts to us that we want to share with you. We ask only that you recognize the pain in yourself or those around you -- and reach out, because no one should have to do it alone.

— Dr. Bonnie Howell, Ithaca, NY, 2012

Table of Contents

NOTE: Each chapter is its own stand-alone meditation and we're with you through each. We've left space with specific intention for your thoughts, feelings, dreams, and concerns. Use them where you find them, and as you are led.

Tell us about them if you wish.

When storm clouds are brewing in your life,
meditation can be a wonderful tool.

Chapter 1

A Brief Introduction to Meditation

To begin each meditation, you must first find a place where you can lie down, or be comfortably seated. There is no magic in choosing; just find a place that's comfortable for you. Make sure that you will be undisturbed for approximately 20 to 30 minutes.

Lie on your back. Relax your shoulders. If you feel any tension or discomfort in your neck, consider using a small neck pillow or roll up a towel to give yourself some support. Your goal is to feel totally relaxed and physically at ease.

Allow your arms to rest at your sides with the palms face up. If seated, rest them on the chair arms. If your arms or legs feel tight, gently roll them side-to-side or shake them to loosen up any tension. Scan your entire body by first tensing and then releasing each body part.

Next, breathe in and out as you focus on your breath completely, perhaps for the first time. Breathe in fully from your abdomen as you feel it rise, and breathe out fully as you feel it fall. Imagine that you have a giant balloon in your abdomen that expands as you inhale and contracts as you exhale. If you are having difficulty feeling this rising and falling, then place your hands on your stomach at the belly button. At first, watch your belly rise and fall with each breath until you feel comfortable with this technique.

Some people feel more relaxed breathing in and out through the nose, while other people prefer to breathe in through the nose and exhale out through the mouth. Experiment with your breathing to find out which type of breathing works best for you.

Each time you wish to meditate, take 10 to 20 smooth, deep breaths in and out so you feel the tension leaving your body, before you begin the meditation. If you practice the technique every day, it will become second nature each time you wish to enter the meditative state. NOW PRACTICE A FEW TIMES.

We believe this ability to relax into ourselves is a natural part of our human makeup, which may get lost and forgotten amidst life's stresses. It is our desire to bring it back as part of our nature; hence, the second meaning to "Meditation by Nature."

If you want to study more about the practice or history of meditation, most public libraries and bookstores have a current selection. You can also find a wealth of information on-line.

LIST A FEW REFERENCE MATERIAL CITATIONS HERE TO PURSUE OVER THE NEXT WEEKS OR MONTHS.

ALSO, NOTE HOW YOU FELT DURING YOUR PRACTICE MEDITATION. WERE YOU COMFORTABLE AND RELAXED OR WERE YOU ANXIOUS? DID YOU FIND YOUR MIND WANDERING OR WERE YOU JUDGING YOUR ABILITY TO 'DO IT RIGHT'? ALL OF THESE ARE NATURAL FOR THE BEGINNING MEDITATOR. I PROMISE IT WILL GET EASIER.

Chapter 2

Meditation On Contemplation

- You may not always have the luxury of a beautiful spot like the one my friend captured.

- However, she has shared it so that you may always have such a place in your mind.

- View, enjoy, visualize and transport yourself into her picture.

- Then make yourself ready to begin the meditation.

CONSIDER:

- How often do we wish we had the time to simply contemplate where we've been, where we are, where we'd like to go from here?

- Often we postpone, digress, and wait for the perfect moment, the perfect spot to engage in that kind of introspection.

- This meditation is designed to help you give yourself permission to find the time, the spot, the inclination right here, right now.

PREPARE YOURSELF:

∾ Begin by finding a spot and position.

∾ Remember: there is no right way, just the way that's right for you.

∾ Close your eyes; don't squeeze them shut, just close them lightly.

∾ Begin your breathing: in to a 3-count, out to a 3-count.

⊰ THE MEDITATION ⊱

∾ Imagine yourself on the beach at sunrise.

∾ It's a glorious morning and you are surprised to find you are the only one in this beautiful spot--the solitude feels like a wonderful vacation from the hubbub of your day-to-day life.

∾ Take off your shoes and feel the damp sand under your feet. Close your eyes and allow the soft morning sun to kiss your face.

∾ What a beautiful spot to contemplate your life!

∾ Ask yourself these questions:
    What do I love about my life today?
    What do I hate?
    What would I change if I could?
    What's stopping me?

∽ As you think about each question, remember to breathe. Begin a 4-count breath if it's comfortable.

∽ Breathe in: one - two - three - four; breathe out: one - two - three - four.

∽ What do I truly love about my life today?

∽ Resolve to remember and be grateful for those parts you truly love.

Now move to the next questions:

∽ What do I hate?

∽ What would I change if I could?

∽ What's standing in my way?

Deal with each question in turn one after the other in the same meditation or if you like as separate meditations.

❧ LEAVING THE MEDITATION ❧

When you are ready, let your breath guide you to a comfortable resting spot.

∽ Breathe in the serenity of this new beginning; breathe out any anxiety left from embarking on unfamiliar territory.

∽ Breathe in the sense of past as servant; breathe out the need for it as master.

- ❧ Breathe in; breathe out; until you are ready to return.

- ❧ Slowly open your eyes.

- ❧ You are exactly where you are supposed to be.

- ❧ Smile.

- ❧ Ready yourself for the next step in the wonderful journey that is your life.

This would be an excellent time to talk about taking notes. Sometimes it's helpful to take some notes right after you finish the meditation. Try it here; we've left some space. Just as thoughts come to you, jot them down; don't censor, judge, edit; just write. These notes will be useful to you later and as you repeat the meditation. If you don't feel up to it, that's okay, too. Maybe the next time you feel called to open this meditation. And if you are led to share, with a friend, a counselor or with us—do so. You'll know when that becomes an important next step.

Chapter 3

Meditation On Depression

No one goes through life without dark periods when:
The future looks bleak and life doesn't seem worth the trouble.
Loneliness and despair appear as the only constant companions.
A sea of personal grief overwhelms every ray of sunshine.

This four-part meditation is designed for use during those distressing and difficult intervals.

NOTES: TAKE A MOMENT BEFORE YOU START TO THINK ABOUT WHAT IS DEPRESSING OR DISTRESSING YOU RIGHT NOW, OR PERHAPS SOMETHING FROM THE PAST. WRITE A FEW NOTES ON THE SUBJECT TO GIVE YOU A STARTING PLACE TO COME BACK TO. IF NO THOUGHTS COME, BEGIN THE MEDITATION AND RETURN TO THIS PLACE AFTER MEDITATING OR AT SOME POINT IN THE FUTURE

It's important to remember there is no shame in seeking help. So if the meditation doesn't bring relief then understand that depression is an illness. So reach out and ask for help; talk to your family physician, counselor, talk to friend or family.

Depression doesn't always go away by itself; so don't try to tough it out and hope it will disappear. Please believe you don't have to do it alone. We don't want that for you.

It might be wise even before you try the meditation to jot down a few people you would be comfortable calling, look up the numbers of local crisis centers, or suicide prevention programs. Keep those numbers here so that they are handy if your depression continues or deepens even after using the meditation.

❧ THE MEDITATION ❧

❧ Close your eyes, just gently. Take a deep breath. Fill your lungs completely with air; hold for a 5-count, then slowly release the air to a count of 5.

❧ As you are breathing in, imagine that you're in the elevator of a tall building; it's a safe, enclosed glass elevator so as you are going up you can look all around you. (Note: If you fear elevators, imagine walking up a gently rising pathway and noticing the changing view as you climb to different levels. Replace the word elevator with pathway each time it's used)

❧ Each time at the top, as you pause your breath, you can see your whole world laid out before you.

❧ Each time notice a different view, a different portion of your life's landscape.

❧ Pay attention to those details that seem particularly troubling, sad, or anxiety provoking. Notice each detail, as you are above it, uninvolved, untouchable from this vantage point.

❧ Breathe in and out; notice how small and far away those details are beginning to appear. Now they begin to seem less significant in the greater landscape that is your life.

✦ THE MEDITATION, PART TWO ✦

∽ Remember, when the elevator ride is over and you get out, you'll have the opportunity to step into any portion of the landscape you choose. It can be present, past, or future.

∽ Now start to imagine, as you go up and down, that your elevator trip is really various phases of your life, past, present, and future. Look around the landscape of your life, choosing a place to visit or revisit once you step out of the elevator. How would you like it to look? Is it a place you know, or a new place just over the horizon?

∽ Are there people there? Do you know them, or are they people you'd like to meet?

∽ How would you like to feel? Have you felt that way before? Is it how you remember it or imagined it?

∽ Begin to prepare yourself for the journey to your chosen landscape.

⊰ THE MEDITATION, PART THREE ⊱

᧥ As you breathe in, imagine now that you've chosen a time and place to visit. Imagine this place is out of the building, and back in your life.

᧥ Look around; notice how comfortable and happy you feel in this place of your choosing, this place of a new beginning. The sky is blue; birds overhead are calling softly to each other against the background of white wispy clouds.

᧥ Get ready to greet the people of your new life. Smile; they are happy to see you.

᧥ Your feeling of belonging gets stronger; you relax, and a sense of peace and joy deeper than you've ever known begins to settle on you. Inhale those feelings.

᧥ As you exhale, release any remaining doubts about the reality of this sacred place, about your ability to reach it, about how you feel.

᧥ Inhale peace and joy. Exhale doubt and sadness.

⊰ THE MEDITATION, PART FOUR ⊱

∽ Enjoy this place as long as you'd like, add detail, feeling, anything you want or need. Keep breathing slowly in and out.

∽ Believe that you will maintain these feelings of joy, peace, and confidence. Resolve to believe that they are a part of you now. You'll carry them with you no matter where you choose to go from your sacred space.

∽ When and only when you are ready, get back into the elevator and prepare to leave the meditation.

∽ Notice each floor going down as you pass it, feeling the joy and peace you've brought along in the anticipation of stepping back into your world. You're poised and ready for your old challenges with new resolve.

∽ Now you're at ground level once again. Stand there for a moment as the doors open. When you feel ready, open your eyes; notice that those positive feelings haven't left you.

∽ You feel relaxed and confident that your life will not overwhelm what you have gained.

∽ Remember the blue-sky picture. Whenever you feel anxious, sad, or afraid, you will look at that picture and be able to return to the sacred space you have chosen in your meditation. It will always be there for you.

Chapter 4

Meditation On Being Alone

Sometimes we are alone by choice, other times by chance. Sometimes we are temporarily alone, and other times it seems as though we'll always be that way. Being alone can be lonely, or it can be a time of creativity and growth.

As those sentences convey, the emotions surrounding aloneness are far from fixed; they may range from sheer bliss to deep depression. This meditation is designed to change the emotion one associates with being alone (if that is the desire.)

☙ THE MEDITATION ❧

∾ Look at the picture of the bird all alone, standing in the water, looking out to sea. Notice detail and color; imagine sounds and smells. Do you feel it's sad that she's all alone, just standing there? Do you identify with her state of mind? Do you wish better for her than such aloneness? Do you wonder . . . where is her partner? Where are the young ones she's brought into the world? Where is the flock?

∾ Fix this living picture in your mind. Close your eyes and begin slow, purposeful breathing, in and out to a 5-count. Now imagine yourself walking on that beach on a beautiful, sunny morning. You are barefoot and the early morning sand is just comfortably warm on your feet. You are without human contact, but far from alone. You notice other creatures coming and going, some in pairs, others in groups, some by themselves. You notice they all seem comfortable regardless of the state of being together or alone. Now you get closer to this one particular bird, standing alone, looking out to sea. Notice how the wind softly ruffles her feathers and the water kisses her toes. She's observing and being.

❧ You are surprised to discover that you can imagine that you understand her as though she was speaking out loud and directly to your soul.

❧ You hear: I am alone, but not lonely. I have purpose and meaning in my life. I have gifts to give to others, but at this moment, I am giving the gift of just being to myself. I don't know how long I will stand here, but I will enjoy this time. I will create a safe haven for my aloneness and rejoice in being comfortable in my own body, my own space, and my own mind.

❧ This is my place in the universe and it was given to me for a reason. I will not question the wisdom of it. It is my safe haven for however long it needs to last. I am happy being here but I will open myself to new possibilities of belonging. My alone time will make me more unguarded, ready, willing to be part of something in addition to myself.

❧ I will be ready for a new partner, friend, group or organization. I will be ready because I am comfortable being alone. One day I will leave here and fly out to meet the horizon.

❧ You listen; you feel the wisdom of her words as you breathe them in with each breath, letting go of those old feelings about being alone as you let each breath out. Her words are your words now, paraphrased so that you will remember them. They are your thoughts now as you breathe in and out. Feelings of comfort and new possibilities empower you. Stay in the meditative state for as long as you want, remembering the picture and the words, enjoying the company.

- When you are ready, start your walk back along the beach. You smile as you remember the lone bird. You feel peaceful, safe, secure, and even joyful. Being alone is not scary, never punishment; it's a state of being and you are comfortable.

- As you walk along, notice the absence of human voice but the cacophony of sounds made by other creatures.

- Let yourself relax into this wonderful place. Breathe it in and hold it just for a moment before letting the breath go. Keep walking, breathing, being.

- Just as you end your walk, you notice that indeed the bird has flown off toward the horizon to seek whatever she may need. She dips her wing toward you as though to say, "We are all right on this solitary journey.

- Because we two are here we are never alone. Imagine me whenever you feel the need and I will come to you in this meditation.'"

- When you are ready, let your eyes slowly open. You are back in your space now, but it feels different. You have contentment; even happiness to share your universe. The thoughts created on your journey are still with you and will remain so.

- Relax, remember, enjoy.

Return to this meditation whenever you find yourself equating being alone with loneliness.

NOTES: HOW DO YOU FEEL ABOUT BEING ALONE RIGHT NOW? BETTER? WORSE? THE SAME?

Chapter 5

Meditation On
Accepting The Unknowable
∾ (Living with Shades of Gray) ∾

Today we are going to meditate about acceptance and presence. In order to be fully present, it is necessary to accept that our choices, our moods, our world will never lay itself out neatly in black and white. Therefore, it is necessary to be present in shades of gray, unknowns, never perfect understanding. Our happiness is found not in waiting for something else to be made clear but in blissfully accepting the gift of the unknown.

TIME TO JOT A FEW NOTES ABOUT THE UNKNOWNS IN YOUR LIFE: DO YOU SPEND A LOT OF YOUR TIME THINKING (WORRYING) ABOUT WHAT MIGHT HAPPEN, WHAT COULD HAPPEN? DO YOU STAY AWAKE AT NIGHT THINKING ABOUT THOSE ISSUES? PUT DOWN GENERAL CATEGORIES OF UNKNOWNS, IF NOT SPECIFICS.

❧ THE MEDITATION ❧

Go back and really look at this picture. It's beautiful, isn't it? Could you be happy here in the midst of all this beauty? Begin your deep breathing with "Yes, I'm happy here," in to a count of 5, out to a count of 10. As you are breathing in this beauty, imagine that you have just been set down here with no information, yet immediately you feel a wonderful sense of calm. Breathe in the beautiful scene. Breathe out your concern over what you don't know. It's perfect, isn't it? Breathe out what you don't yet know, one statement at a time:

- I don't know what day it is.

- I don't yet know whether it's almost morning, or nearly night.

- I don't know whether the sky is clearing or a storm is brewing on the horizon.

- I don't know if I will walk alone on the beach or perhaps meet someone along the way.

- I don't know whether I am safe here. If there are people, will they be friend or foe?

Softly acknowledge that you would usually be anxious with so many unknowns.

Breathe in, then breathe out and say to yourself: I am often uncomfortable with so many unknowns, so many shades of gray, but I will trust I am where I am supposed to be even as my mind asks:

∽ Should I seek shelter?

∽ Should I run from this place?

∽ Should I cry for help?

∽ Will anyone hear me if I do?

But today you know your breathing protects you. You don't need immediate answers to any of those questions. Breathe in the beauty. Know that you are safe here for this time. You have everything you need. Shelter is just down the beach if you need it. You know where you are and help is available if you ask for it. Breathe in the beauty and safety; breathe out the concerned questions of your fearful mind.

❦ LEAVING THE MEDITATION ❧

❧ Turn around and see your own footprints in the sand. Notice that your footprints are also in shades of gray.

❧ You realize that you've made it safely on your journey despite not knowing all the information you'd usually like to know.

❧ You have had good and bad surprises, but here you are safe in this moment of total presence.

❧ Stand here for a minute and breathe in this knowledge. Breathe out self-doubt. Breathe in your ability to live in the moment without perfect information. Breathe out the need for black and white.

❧ Breathe in the wonderful shades of gray in your life. Acknowledge and embrace them. Keep breathing, in to a count of 5, out to a count of 5. When all the anxiety related to the unknown seems to have left your body, leave the meditation.

❧ You feel wonderfully relaxed and accepting, knowing your footprints from past, present and future are in shades of gray. Know that any time you feel anxious in the moment, you may return to the meditation and re-establish your sense of peace with your circumstances.

❧ THOUGHTS, FEELINGS, EMOTIONS ON SHADES OF GRAY ❧

TRY NOW TO IDENTIFY THE UNKNOWNS THAT STRESS YOU TODAY. WHERE ARE THE SHADES OF GRAY THAT TROUBLE YOU? ARE YOU ABLE TO LET GO AS YOU DO THE MEDITATION? WRITE THEM FOR YOU; SHARE THEM WITH US IF YOU WISH.

Chapter 6

Meditation On Letting Go

So many things at so many times in our life come to us, and then move on, with or without our permission.

WHAT ARE THEY IN YOUR LIFE?

❧ WHY LET GO? ❧

Only you will know what led you to this meditation. We can only offer, solely as encouragement, what letting go is not.

- ❧ To let go is not to forget or to ignore.

- ❧ Letting go does not negate feelings of love, anger, regret, pain or loss, though it may involve overcoming all of those things.

- ❧ It is not about winning or losing, pride or prejudice, gain or loss.

If it is none of these things, then why is it one of the most difficult tasks for a human being to accomplish?

⊰ LETTING GO OF WHERE WE'VE BEEN ⊱

To let go is to leave the place we know, no matter how painful it is or has become, and move out, usually alone, to embark on a journey in the great unknown. It may produce feelings of anxiety, sadness, and loneliness, or at the very least a general feeling of discontent. We look at our world as no longer a comfortable space in which to dwell. We know it's time to move on, but how?

The purpose of this meditation is to help you in that journey, by learning to cherish memories, to be thankful for the experiences that made you laugh and made you cry. It's about all that you have, all that you will have and how you will grow through the transitional experience. Letting go takes the courage to accept change and the strength to move on to uncharted territory. To let go is to open a door and clear a path to set you free.

❧ PAUSING TO ASSESS WHERE WE ARE ❧

∽ PREPARING FOR THE MEDITATION ∽

∽ Find a comfortable spot where you are not likely to be disturbed for a half hour or so.

∽ Find a comfortable position—there is no right or wrong, only comfortable.

∽ Close your eyes; don't squeeze them shut, just close them gently.

∽ Breathe in and out, first to a 3-count. Breathe in: one - two - three; breathe out: one - two - three.

∽ Gradually deepen your breath; if it's comfortable, try for a 4-count. In one - two - three – four. Out one - two - three - four.

∽ THE MEDITATION ∽

∽ Begin by deeply feeling what led you to this meditation. Don't judge or fight the feelings. Let them consume you just for a moment. Can you name the feelings? Is there fear or anger, despondency, hopelessness? Or is it apathy, world-weariness, boredom that comes to mind?

∽ Now begin your breathing. You've found a count comfortable for you now. Breathe in the sense of wanting to chart new territory; breathe out the need to hang on to what you know.

∽ Breathe in the sense of adventure you've had in discovering new places, new people; breathe out the burden of hanging on to what no longer serves your purpose today.

ꝏ As you breathe, know that you don't have to demonize what has been in order to let go. Cherish those memories and take comfort that memories will always be there if you need them again.

ꝏ Breathe in the knowledge that you don't have to know what will replace that which you let go. Whatever that new path may be will be exactly right for where you are today. Notice that you don't have to see exactly what's ahead, to know it's the right path for you today.

❧ TAKING THE DIMLY LIGHTED
PATH TO OUR FUTURE ❧

Acknowledge that change can be wonderful and exciting as well as fear provoking.

Trust the rightness of your need, your right, to begin again, several times a day if necessary.

Acknowledge your fears of the unknown. Can you name them, if so write them here. Even general categories will help you clear the way.

∞ Keep breathing in and out as you walk along the path. Notice the sun on the horizon; notice the water; smell it; hear it; feel it as you walk.

∞ Breathe in the changing sameness of the water—it is always there, but always changing, creating a new shoreline path. Breathe out the need to know what's next; breathe in the calm security of the rightness of the new path.

∞ Feel your feet as they gently make new footprints in the sand. Turn around and look back if you want to. Trust that moving forward is right for you. Know you are where your footprints have brought you; they represent all you are and all you have been; they've made you ready for the new journey.

ॐ Letting go of the past that's no longer needed doesn't mean forgetting; it only means letting it serve you on the new path.

ॐ Breathe one - two - three - four. What do I dislike about my life? Are those things temporary or permanent? Are they of my own making or the result of a relationship to someone or something else? Which of these am I resigned to or feel can't be changed?

ॐ Breathe to a count of four. Which would I change if I could? Breathe to a count of four (or slower if it's more comfortable). What are the things I could change and haven't? Breathe as slowly as is comfortable. Ask "What's stopping me from making those changes?"

ॐ Imagine yourself having made each of those changes. Are you happier, calmer? Is there less stress in your life? Hold that answer and breathe it in and out, gently taking in the happiness, and the serenity of change, breathing out the blocks to the change you truly want to make. Stay as long as you like in the meditative state of accepting change in your life.

❧ LEAVING THE MEDITATION ❧

~ When you are ready, allow your breath to slowly return to a normal in-and-out state (1-count.) Keep your eyes closed and begin to imagine a new day. Change is possible; change will make your life happier and less stressful.

~ Contemplate the first change you will make in this new day. Hold it in your thoughts as you slowly open your eyes.

~ You are alert and rested; you look at the last picture to remind you that a new day is dawning on your life. You look forward to it and know that as you are ready to make additional changes, you may contemplate them again here.

❧ A NEW DAY DAWNING ❧

NOW THINK ABOUT YOUR NEW DAY:

PERHAPS A FEW RESOLUTIONS MIGHT HELP YOU REMEMBER WHERE YOU WANT TO BE AND WHO YOU WANT TO BE IN THIS NEW DAY.

JOT THEM HERE:

Chapter 7

Meditation On Addiction

◄[INTRODUCTION]►

A s my friend and I were contemplating the next in our series of meditations, life, as it is wont to do, kept happening.

Sadly, a great talent (and a suffering human being) passed away, and in her passing gave us inspiration.

When some said we should not honor her because she was a drug addict, we cried for her and for all the others who are suffering or who have suffered because of this sad illness.

The next signal indicating the rightness of this path was the photographer part of our team "happening" upon this next picture.

Is it inappropriate to get inspiration from death? If this helped even one person find a way to short change this life-ending disease, I'm convinced Whitney would take great comfort and would know that we seek to honor her.

❧ END OF THE ROAD ❧

"Is this picture too graphic, too dark, for a meditation?" the photographer asked. For one in the grasp of addiction there can be no such thing as too dark. And graphic it must be in order to communicate the story.

We could give you the statistics: how many dead, how many lives ruined. We could tell you addiction ends up in one of three ways: institutions, jail or death. Those are the only choices. And it doesn't matter who you are or what you've done or haven't done.

Only you will know when you are ready for this meditation; only you will know when you are in need of inspiration outside yourself. And you will know when the bottom has risen up to meet you and taken nearly all that you have. Our prayers, our thoughts, our good wishes are with you.

❧ THE MEDITATION ❧

❧ Get into comfortable clothes.

❧ Find a quiet place where no one or nothing is likely to inter-
rupt.

❧ Close your eyes lightly and relax your muscles.

❧ Begin breathing in and out, slowly and comfortably; then
let your breath deepen. In to a count of three, out to a
count of three. Then, if you are ready, to a count of four, in
and out.

❧ Breathe in as much peace as you can allow; breathe out
self-hatred, humiliation, and grief.

❧ Breathe in the force of all who have loved you; breathe out
the quiet desperation that lives with you every day.

❧ Breathe in the good and decent human being you are;
breathe out the bad things you may have done, the embar-
rassment you feel.

❧ Breathe in the feeling that there is a benevolent being that
cares about you; breathe out your loneliness and isolation.

❧[YOU FEEL AS THOUGH YOU ARE HERE]☙

In the depths of your addiction, this is your life view, Turn the page, look at the picture, is this how life currently appears to you.

- ❧ This world looks dark and forbidding, the waves facing you high and dangerous.

- ❧ The cloud that stands between you and the rest of your life seems too insurmountable. You are without hope.

- ❧ Yes, others see the sun just beyond the cloud; they see the lovely ocean scene. You do not.

- ❧ And because you cannot see beyond the darkness, the drink, the joint, the pill call to you and promise relief.

- ❧ Your experience tells you that relief is very temporary and then you are faced with an even darker life picture.

- ❧ Try for a moment to iimagine a new possibility, let your meditative practice and your imagination allow for the possibility of a new picture.

❦ IMAGINE YOU ARE HERE ❧

Turn the page, look at this picture, see yourself looking at it's possibilities. The world hasn't magically changed into a shiny new reality, not yet. Just start by seeing the clouds beginning to liift,, the sun breaking through. Imagine the picture of hope.

- ❧ Where you are, there is no sun, only darkness, only pain and suffering. We know this place and we've come to help you.

- ❧ Walk with us for a while; imagine that we are there with you; imagine us in any form you choose---but know that you are not alone.

- ❧ Talk to us; tell us whatever is on your mind and in your heart. We have heard it and it does not frighten or repel us.

- ❧ We will help you see that the sun is just over the horizon. You only have to look and believe that it is there. Just for right now, just for the next half hour, just for today.

- ❧ Breathe with us. Choose with us. Breathe out the addiction and its pain; breathe in life and all that it can be.

- ❧ Let your breath be as slow as possible now, even to a count of 5 if you are able. This is difficult work, but we are here to guide you.

- ❧ As you begin to see the sun over the horizon, rejoice. Breathe in the joy; breathe out the pain. Keep breathing until you are sure that sunrise is there.

❧ ENDING THE MEDITATION ❧

- When you are ready, gradually let your breathing return to normal. Don't hurry; stay and let it happen slowly and naturally.

- Open your eyes. You feel relaxed and at peace. You enjoy that feeling and want to keep it.

- The addictive substance no longer holds power over you. Call someone, share it, seek help for follow-up if you'd like. There are many programs, where like-minded people will not judge you or berate you. They will offer their love and support. Call one of us, if nothing else comes to mind. We will share your journey.

Chapter 8

Meditation On Loss

My friends and I recently took a trip to visit NYC. On our way there, we talked about the meditations that we'd still like to write.

A consensus developed around the word 'Loss' and the many different kinds of loss — people, things, abilities, interests — all of which can walk out of our lives, usually without notice, losses for which we don't always have adequate time to plan. We had all used the analogy of footprints in the sand. And then the conversation was set aside until after our vacation weekend.

Although the meditations were put on hold, the process continued, unbeknownst to us at the time.

Empty Sky Monument
Remembering New Jersey Residents Lost On
September 11th, 2001

❧ INTRODUCTION: THE VISIT COMMEMORATING LOSS ❧

We had not planned to visit the memorial that day; we just happened upon it while exploring Liberty Park. Walking through the walls of names etched in stainless steel, we did not know anyone and were not looking for anyone in particular, but my eyes were drawn to a single name: Wanda Green. I said, "I wonder what Wanda Green was doing that day. I wonder what was lost for her that day."

When I returned home, I looked up Wanda on the Internet. She was a flight attendant who wasn't even supposed to be flying that day. She was 49 years old, a single parent of two children to whom she gave pajamas for Christmas every year. (I do that with my kids, too.) Her parents were expecting her arrival in California. They confirmed the visit by phone the night before — the last time they would ever speak to her.

Photo By Barbara Warland

That last part — "the last time they would ever speak to her" — filled me with such a profound sense of loss I could not adequately describe it, but in that moment this thought came instantly and clearly to mind:

What if we knew each time we did something that it was the last time we would ever do it? Not just big stuff like Wanda's telephone call, or the last time I'd speak to my Dad before he died, but little stuff, too. Things like the last time you'd ever play golf or tennis, or in my case, wind surf or run a 5K. For whatever reason it was the last time, and you didn't know. The last time you'd drop your kids at day care or high school before they graduated and moved on. The last time...

Would we want to know it was the last time? If we did know would we remember it better? Enjoy it more? Change it just a little? Say more, or say less?

I think the idea of having that knowledge would be so agonizingly heartbreaking, it would be beyond a human being's ability to endure.

Yet we often grieve by remembering those parts of our loss we'd like to have handled better or done differently; changed a little or a lot. Does it help? Only to a point. Once that point has been reached, we invite the use of this meditation.

YOU MIGHT WANT TO JOT A FEW NOTES ABOUT THE LOSS OR LOSSES YOU'D LIKE TO CONCENTRATE ON IN THIS MEDITATION.

◄ THE MEDITATION ►

໑ Find a comfortable spot, sitting or lying, where you are not likely to be interrupted for a half hour or so. Begin your breathing naturally at first, and then deepen the breaths to a count of three, then four.

໑ Experience your loss from this perspective: "If I had known, what would I have done differently?" What would I change? What differences would those changes have made? None, a few, a lot?

໑ Accept that you did not know, that you did the best you could. Forgive yourself if you did not do the best you think you could have. You are human, and we humans can see only the past, not the future.

໑ Breathe in your acceptance that some moments are gone forever; breathe out your regret.

໑ Breathe in your beautiful memories about what's lost.

໑ Breathe out your guilt, your grief that you did not make it the perfect moment.

∾ Breathe in your knowledge that each moment comes and goes, and we never know which will be the last one exactly like it.

∾ Breathe out the desire to change what's past.

∾ Breathe in the sincere intention to enjoy each future moment as though it may be the last ......

∾ Breathe out this moment with no regret, this time of reflection.

∾ Breathe in your desire to leave nothing unsaid, undone, unloved.

∾ Breathe out the sadness of last moments; breathe in the opportunity of making moments last.

⚜ ENDING THE MEDITATION ⚜

∾ Keep breathing in and out, deep breaths, for as long as you need in order to hold the grief of your loss and then let it go. There is no right length of time; just take what you need.

∾ When you are ready, let your breathing naturally return to normal. Open your eyes and look around. You are rested; you are content. You have acknowledged your loss and will forever hold it in your heart.

∾ You will let it be in its proper place in your life, but you will be able to move on and enjoy those moments yet to come.

∾ We are all only footprints in the sand, here for a short time. Our lives are a series of moments, some remarkable, some not so, but all only moments.

∾ If we turn around to judge where we've been, the footprints are already starting to disappear.

∾ Look forward, for we can only change what is there.

∾ Vow to live each moment as the last; we promise it will make a difference in how you see and live your life.

WE REALIZE THIS WAS A DIFFICULT MEDITATION. WHAT ARE YOUR FEELINGS AND THINKING ABOUT LOSS IN YOUR LIFE? COULD YOU TAKE A FEW MOMENTS TO WRITE ABOUT THEM HERE? INCLUDE THOSE LOSSES YOU'D LIKE TO CONCENTRATE ON THE NEXT TIME YOU ARE CALLED TO COMPLETE THIS MEDITATION.

ONCE YOU'VE COMPLETED THAT PROCESS, USE THE NEXT PAGE TO LIST THOSE PEOPLE, PLACES, THINGS YOU'D LIKE TO ACKNOWLEDGE AND REMEMBER BECAUSE THEY ARE STILL IN YOUR LIFE AND VOW NOT TO TAKE ANY MOMENT WITH THEM FOR GRANTED.

Chapter 9

Meditation on the Acceptance of Joy

❧ INTRODUCTION TO ACCEPTING JOY ❧

I t seems an odd concept at first: Why would I have to meditate on welcoming happiness into my life? Joy should be accepted naturally, without question; it should come easily. Yet many of my clients and friends have reported that it's not as easy and straightforward as it might seem. I find myself in agreement with them.

What is your reaction? How do you feel when life events bring those things that should offer joy, happiness, and contentment to you? Aha, I introduced the word "should" and that word changes everything, does it not? This subject came to me; I discussed it with Charlotte and asked her to think about it with her photographic mind-set. She came back to me with a set of pictures that brought the meditation to fruition.

Beauty, joy, and harmony -- it's all around us. Perhaps it's even the natural state of things. What, then, keeps us from accepting that state of mind in our own life? Let me offer some possibilities

෯ Mistrust: This can't be happening in my life; good things never happen. It's a temporary state so I won't get used to it. If I do get used to it, it will surely disappear, because nothing good ever lasts.

෯ Fear: Mistrust's loyal companion. I'm afraid it won't last and I'll just be disappointed. I'll end up worse off than I was before. If you love something too much it will be taken away. If you are too happy, you're just asking for trouble.

෯ Guilt: Perhaps the heart of it. I don't deserve to be happy; I'm a screw up; I've done a lot of bad things and let people down. I can't possibly be allowed to be joyful. The universe just simply doesn't work that way. It wouldn't be right if it did.

Does that pretty much summarize the way you feel about joy? If so, please join us in this meditation.

NOTES: JUST A FEW TO CAPTURE THOSE THINGS YOU ARE JOYOUS ABOUT, THOSE THINGS YOU CHERISH, AND THOSE THINGS ABOUT YOUR LIFE THAT DELIGHT YOU. YOU'LL BE SURPRISED AT HOW MANY THERE ARE, AND HOW MANY YOU'LL ADD AS YOU THINK ABOUT IT AND ACCEPT YOUR OWN WORTHINESS TO FEEL JOYOUS.

⊰ THE MEDITATION ⊱

- Look at this picture in all of its glorious detail. The bird has a home, food, peace, and a beautiful day.

- Can you imagine it joyful, in harmony with its surroundings, comfortable and at peace? Watchful, yes, but not fearful.

- Do you think the bird experiences guilt for its good fortune? Does it pause to conjure up what might happen tomorrow or the day after?

- Or does it accept all that is with heartfelt gratitude?

- Let's pledge to accept the joy in our lives from that perch.

❧ PREPARING FOR THE MEDITATION ❧

∽ Close your eyes; don't squeeze them shut, just close them gently. Breathe in and out, first to a count of three.

∽ Gradually deepen your breath; if it's comfortable, try for a four-count. In one - two - three - four, out one - two - three - four.

∽ Find a comfortable position—there is no right or wrong, only comfortable.

∽ Breathe in this understanding: life is designed to be lived joyfully. Your life need not be an exception.

∽ Breathe out the guilt that you are human and have not lived perfectly.

∽ Breathe in your trust of the rightness of pleasure in your being and vow to hold that belief in your heart.

∽ Breathe out the fear that happiness cannot last and relish the joyous feeling of the here and now.

∽ Breathe in the sincere intention to appreciate each moment for as long as it lasts, unspoiled by fear, guilt or lack of trust.

∽ Breathe out the desire to live in a neutral zone; embrace the joyous life lived to the best of your abilities.

∽ Breathe in the acceptance that we are all good enough.

- We had good enough parents,

- We have been a good enough parent, partner, friend, son or daughter.

- This is my rightful place in the great scheme of things and for that I am good enough just as I am.

❧ I ACCEPT MY JOYOUS PLACE IN THE UNIVERSE BECAUSE I AM ❧

❧ ENDING THE MEDITATION ❧

↬ Keep breathing in and out, deep breaths for as long as you need to allow joyfulness to take residence in your heart. There is no right length of time; just take what you need.

↬ When you are ready, let your breathing naturally return to normal. Open your eyes and look around. You are rested; you are content; you are joyful.

↬ You live knowing you are worthy. You can live without fear of happiness. You can trust its rightful place in your life.

↬ Vow to live each moment of enjoyment with as much enthusiasm and acceptance as any other emotion that comes into your life.

↬ This is your rightful place in the universe of persons and all else that lives and breathes on this earth. Accept it, and by all means enjoy it. It's not earned; it's given.

↬ Go back to really look at the picture. Is it beautiful in its entirety? Ugly in its specifics?

↬ Do you know what lies beneath the surface?

↬ Is it full of life or in the process of dying?

∽ How you see it says more about you than the picture.

∽ We are all creatures of the universe: beautiful, ugly, alive, dying.

∽ Enjoy this time and this place. Jot a few notes about your worthiness.

∽ Then write a few notes about what is joyous in your life and vow to accept it.

❧ I AM WORTHY BECAUSE I AM: ON THE USE OF THIS BOOK ❧

Such a simple concept but so difficult, even impossible, for many of us to believe.. We hope this meditation, in combination with some of the others and whatever outside help you may need will bring you closer and closer to accepting the truth of this little statement.

You might think this silly, but if you have a picture of yourself, paste it here and remember this is a picture of a good person, open to changing and growing and helping others do the same. However, this person is already worthy just as they are, without doing or changing anything. Send us your picture by e-mail and we promise to accept you, even love you, until you can do so yourself.

JUST AS I AM; WORTHY IN EVERY WAY

Our words and pictures are meant to be used over and over again, as new issues come up or return. Sometimes you may feel yourself slipping back emotionally around one or more of the meditative issues. Time for a short refresher course? Do the meditation, read your notes. We KNOW that what you have gained will not disappear. It may only need to be awakened once again.

The set is also designed to be shared with someone else who might benefit. It may be a vehicle for you to reach out to someone in need when you sense they might be open to receive. You will know when it is right for you to share—we promise. Just being there is oft times the most important part of helping someone else. That presence may be silent, or it may be accompanied by words of encouragement, understanding, and hope-- but seldom advice. You may choose to read the meditation aloud to them, or meditate with them. The book is a tool to help you open the door of presence.

ON THE OTHER HAND, this little manuscript may lie still sometimes and just be enjoyed for its beautiful photography— perhaps on a bedside stand, coffee table, or desktop. From there it may be noticed and called up to be useful in a deeper way yet again.

Please share your comments and suggestions; this is an ever-expanding community of souls and we all need you.

FOR NOW, THE END: This is only a temporary ending, of course. There will be more meditations as subjects come up or new insights are brought to us. Please offer us your suggestions; we will be grateful for them.

Bonnie and Charlotte

SPACE FOR THOUGHTS, FEELINGS, EMOTIONS, THINGS YOU WANT TO SHARE AGAIN WITH YOURSELF OR WITH OTHERS. BLESS YOUR WILLINGNESS TO OPEN YOUR HEART, AND IF NEED BE YOUR ARMS TO ADDRESS HUMAN SUFFERING WHEREVER YOU FIND IT—STARTING WITH INSIDE YOURSELF.

FINALLY, ON THESE LAST FEW PAGES WE'VE LEFT ROOM FOR YOU TO HELP US WITH THE NEXT EDITION. WE ASK WITH ALL HUMILITY AND SINCERITY; WHAT SUBJECTS, ISSUES, CONCERNS DO YOU WISH HAD BEEN ADDRESSED BUT WERE NOT? JOT THEM DOWN AND WRITE US AT *BHHCMC@YAHOO.COM.*

Made in the USA
Charleston, SC
24 February 2016